invitation to ART

By SHIRLEY HOCHMAN

STERLING PUBLISHING CO., INC.   NEW YORK

Oak Tree Press Co., Ltd. London & Sydney

OTHER BOOKS OF INTEREST

Alkema's Complete Guide to Creative Art for Young People

Aluminum and Copper Tooling

Aquarelle and Watercolor Complete

Bridgman's Complete Guide to Drawing from Life

Calder's Animal Sketching

Carlson's Guide to Landscape Painting

Complete Crayon Book

Constructive Anatomy

Crafting with Nature's Materials

Creative Claywork

Creative Paper Crafts in Color

Decoupage: Simple & Sophisticated

Drafting Techniques for the Artist

Drawing from Nature

Exhibit Methods

Express Yourself in Drawing

Family Book of Crafts

Ideas for Collage

Identifying Art

Junk Sculpture

Lithographic Prints from Stone & Plate

Mosaics with Natural Stones

Painting Abstract Landscapes

Postercraft

Potato Printing

Practical Encyclopedia of Crafts

Prints—from Linoblocks, Woodcuts, etc.

Screen Printing

Sculpture for Beginners

Sculpturing with Wax

Stained Glass Crafting

Tole Painting

Whittling and Wood Carving

Copyright © 1974 by Sterling Publishing Co., Inc.
419 Park Avenue South, New York, N.Y. 10016
British edition published by Oak Tree Press Co., Ltd., Nassau, Bahamas
Distributed in Australia and New Zealand by Oak Tree Press Co., Ltd.,
P.O. Box J34, Brickfield Hill, Sydney 2000, N.S.W.
Distributed in the United Kingdom and elsewhere in the British Commonwealth
by Ward Lock Ltd., 116 Baker Street, London W 1
Manufactured in the United States of America
All rights reserved
Library of Congress Catalog Card No.:73-93593
Sterling ISBN 0-8069-5292-X Trade   Oak Tree 7061-2481-2
5293-8 Library

Contents

Collection, Villagonzalo, Madrid.
"SELF PORTRAIT," Goya.

An Invitation

Have you ever felt that no one has ever shared your ideas and feelings? Art may help you to overcome this lonely feeling. You may find that many paintings made both long years ago and today show ideas and feelings just like your own. This whole book is an invitation to discover your own ideas and create your own images in art.

Art is an adventure in seeing. You can "read" a story in paintings. You can "meet" people who lived long ago and see exactly how they looked and how they lived. But art is not only about the past. It is also about new ideas. It is even about you—what you think and feel about yourself, your friends, and your world.

Looking at works of art will help you to understand what artists have to say about people, places, and things. Creating your own art will help you to explore your own ideas about these things. This book is about seeing art and creating art. We hope that you will enjoy your seeing and doing and that you will discover new ways to look at art.

One of the most exciting things about art is the fact that no one can tell you what *you* should think. Your personal ideas and feelings are the important things. You cannot be told how you must feel about art any more than you can be told how you must feel about yourself. However, sharing your ideas about art and listening to the ideas of others help you to get the most out of an art experience.

Some works of art are easy to "read." Others take time to understand. Still others will not have any meaning for you. Only you will know what you like. When you are asked, express your honest opinion. The works of art illustrated in this book will encourage you to think about art, to talk about art, and to create art of your own.

Your ideas about art may begin to change as you read, look at reproductions of paintings and drawings, study original works of art, and exchange ideas with other people. Your appreciation and enjoyment will grow if you take the first and only required step—accept our invitation to open your eyes to art!

THE GALLERY VISIT

Look at the pictures in this book as you would look at paintings in a gallery. Stop longer in front of those that interest you most. Notice what the painting is about. Guess at reasons why the artist might have painted in such a manner. When you search for ideas in art, you do more than just pass by—you are really opening your eyes to art. One of the advantages of having this "art gallery in a book" is that you can easily return and view the paintings again and again. Great works of art and famous artists will become familiar and invite you to continue discovering art.

ALIKE AND DIFFERENT

Comparing paintings can be a key to understanding works of art. You can discover ways in which paintings are alike and ways in which they are different. Can you find two pictures in this book that are alike because they both show the artists' views of a street? Look for the ways in which these two paintings are different. What other paintings are alike in one way and different in another? It is fun to make these discoveries for yourself.

DISCOVER DESIGN

Exploring art will help you to understand design and beauty. You will discover that artists create their designs by using lines, shapes, colors, light and dark, space, movement, mass, variety and repetition. You can use these same ideas in *your* creative designs. You may want to try some of the suggested activities or you may invent your own ways to create art.

Line

Lines are used to express ideas. Notice the way they suggest motion in "Forces of a Street" by Umberto Boccioni on page 37. The simple "tricks" on the right may show you how line can be used to fool your eyes.

Try This

With pencil, crayon or soft-tipped ink marker, make a design using many different lines. Fill the paper with your ideas.

Next, make lines to show your ideas of rain,

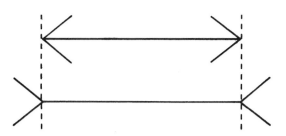

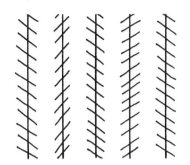

The lines are the same length, but one seems shorter. Why?

The straight up-and-down lines seem to lean because of the slanting lines that cross them.

wind, fast, slow. Look at the lines in "Puppet Show" by Paul Klee on page 21. Notice how this artist used the same lines and different lines to express his ideas.

Shape

A shape is formed by a line or lines. Shapes can describe people, places, or things that you recognize, or they may be just shapes. What kind of shapes can you find in "Puppet Show" on page 21? In "Woman with Mango" on page 33?

Try This

Use crayon or paint to design shapes that have no name. Fill your paper, repeating the same shapes and changing the size of the shapes. Try connecting the shapes with lines. Notice the striped patterns on the shapes in

"Puppet Show." Can you invent a pattern? Use it to make the shapes you have designed more attractive.

Space

One way to show deep space on a flat paper is to use what is called perspective. Simple perspective shows lines that seem to disappear in the distance. The point where all the lines seem to meet and disappear is called the "vanishing point."

Notice the lines in "Café Terrace at Night" by Vincent van Gogh on page 25. Lines that suggest the road, the café floor, café windows, and café awning follow the rules of perspective. However, Van Gogh, like most artists, used the rules of perspective freely. Look at the pictures in this book, and decide which of the artists wanted to give the feeling of deep space and which were interested in the "flat" design of the painting.

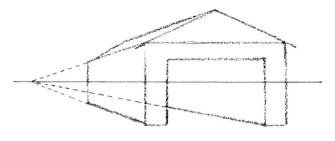

Vanishing point.

Try This

Draw a line and decide where the vanishing point will be. Using a ruler, make a series of lines that meet at that point. The lines you make might suggest train tracks, a road, a row of buildings, or a design. Then add lines to make your choice clear, or add lines and shapes to make your design more interesting.

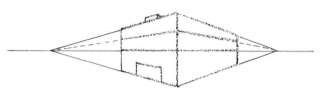

A building seen from the corner seems to go back to two vanishing points.

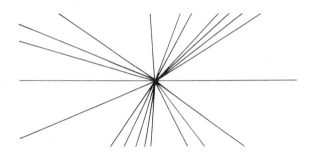

Movement

Lines and shapes can be used to show movement. Notice the motion in "Forces of a Street" on page 37. Today, artists may paint floating shapes and masses of tangled lines. Movement may be the main idea in the painting. In our lives, we experience so many different kinds of movement that it is easy to see why artists are interested in picturing it.

Try This

Use a soft-tipped ink marker to make a pattern suggesting the movement of a storm, snow, or waves.

Mass

Mass is the solid form suggested in paintings by the use of light and shadow. Some painters make their work appear thick, round and solid. Others like flat shapes. You will see mass or roundness in most of the pictures in this book. Hold an egg, apple, or ball near a light and notice the way the lights and shadows change around the form.

Try This

Use a very soft pencil to draw real or imaginary rocks. Arrange the rocks according to the "rule" of perspective. The rule simply is that the rocks farthest away from you seem smaller and will be higher on your paper. Now, make the rocks seem heavy by adding dark shadows.

Variety and Repetition

Artists find that repeating the same thing can be boring. Therefore, they often use a variety of shapes, lines, colors, and textures. But artists sometimes purposely repeat certain shapes, lines, colors, and textures. They often aim for a balance between repetition and variety. You may examine a work of art and decide whether or not the artist used variety or repetition, or both.

Try This

Use a crayon and a large sheet of paper, and write or print your name in as many different ways as possible: in capital letters, small letters, slanted (italic) letters, and so on. Repeat the letters that you find interesting. Make a design of your name. As you write your name in different ways, you create variety. As you repeat certain letters to make the over-all design more interesting, you use repetition.

Color

Through color, artists can express moods, feelings, and ideas. Notice the pale colors in "Rouen Cathedral" by Claude Monet on page 13. Contrast these colors with the solid, dark, and rich colors in "Don Manuel" by Francisco

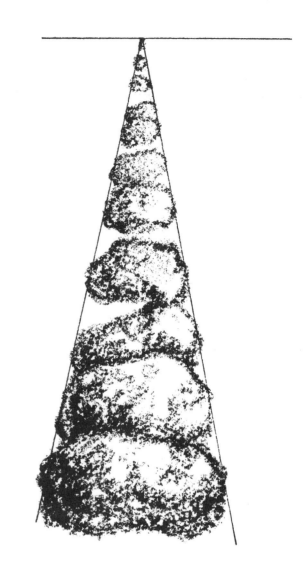

Goya on page 29. Color is one of the first things we notice about a painting.

Dark and Light

Dark and light colors help make ideas clear. Color contrasts can tell a story. Notice the dark and light colors in "Don Manuel." If you look at a painting through half-closed eyes, the dark and light pattern of the colors will become clearer.

Try This

Place a piece of white chalk on a white paper. Observe the chalk carefully. Now, place the same piece of chalk on a piece of black paper. When could you see the chalk more clearly? Why? How does what you observed about contrast and clarity compare with the use of the background colors in "Don Manuel"?

7

"View of Toledo," El Greco
1548–1614

Toledo was the city in Spain where El Greco lived. It was a place of wonder and it was also a place of fear and mystery. As you study this picture you may be able to understand some of the artist's feelings. The stormy sky has strange shapes. The contrasting light and dark colors demand your attention.

Now, look down on the city. The curves of the hills, road and stream seem to twist and turn upwards towards the heart of the city. The great steeple of the cathedral and the grey stone castle stand out against the dark sky. Imagine yourself as a wanderer, climbing the lonely path, crossing the bridge and finally arriving at the cathedral.

This view shows the city of Toledo, but El Greco did not paint it *exactly* as the ordinary person saw the city. The scene was changed by the ideas and imagination of the artist. The colors give a special mood to the painting. Notice the greens and blues that show the natural landscape. Yet, El Greco did not copy Nature. He created a work of art. Notice how the light seems to come from the sky and touch the buildings and the hills.

People are pictured in this landscape, but they are very small. It is as though El Greco was not interested in their everyday activities. The "View of Toledo" is about the lasting wonder of a great city which the artist has made great for all time.

The moving forms, the rich dark colors, the serious mood of this painting are the special mark of this artist. Perhaps this picture will help you to begin to get an idea of the mood El Greco could create in his art.

It is interesting to think about the feelings this painting brings forth. Does it suggest powers that are greater than men? Why are men pictured very small and Nature made so powerful? Why do people find this a very serious picture? Do you like to look at it? Do you wonder why?

In other paintings, El Greco made human figures taller than they appeared in real life. His landscapes too, seem to travel upwards. This gives an elegant, flamelike and spiritual feeling to his work. The manner in which El Greco used shapes to show feeling and mood places him in line with many painters of today. They create shapes to show personal ideas. Sometimes the shapes in modern art cannot be recognized. El Greco's paintings always picture his world in a way that is easily recognized.

El Greco pictured saints and churchmen with great feeling. His painted figures seem to turn and reach upwards towards the sky. They show the mysteries of the world. His

Frick Collection, New York.

"ST. JEROME"

Painted about 1604-1614. 47¾ × 42¾ in. (121 × 109 cm.). Oil on Canvas. Metropolitan Museum of Art. Bequest of Mrs. H. O. Havemeyer, 1939. The H. O. Havemeyer Collection.

"VIEW OF TOLEDO," El Greco.

Escorial, Madrid.

"ST. MAURICE AND THE THEBAN LEGION"

work has a deeply religious feeling. This same mood is shown in the stormy skies he pictured. El Greco is famous for the special quality of his skies.

Some people say that El Greco had poor eyesight and actually saw the world in an unusual way. Other people say that the artist changed shapes on purpose in order to express his own feelings. We will never know about El Greco's eyesight but there is no question about his skill and the lasting appeal of his work.

Try This

El Greco pictured an ancient city on a hill. Imagine a city on a hill. Think of its buildings, towers, churches, castles, homes, barns, and other buildings.

Use a soft-tipped marker to make a sketch

of this imaginary place. Start with rectangles of different sizes. Have some of the rectangles overlap.

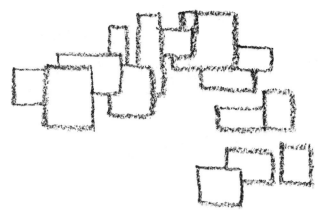

Now add arches, towers, windows and doors in a variety of shapes. Curved lines and circles may suggest sculpture or architectural details.

Now add the hills. Your work should not look like the El Greco. Try to make a sketch that is about your ideas and inventions.

10

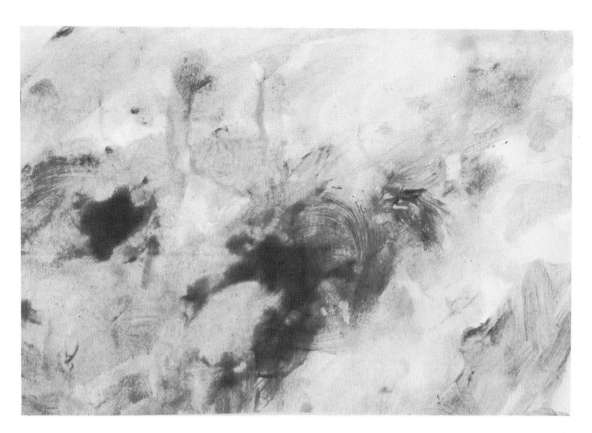

Try This

Create a stormy sky. Do not copy the sky in the painting. However, the painting may help you to feel a storm and get into a stormy mood. As you think about the sky you will picture, use your hand to repeat the motion of wind, rain, and clouds.

Now wet a piece of paper. The wet paper will help your color to flow into cloudlike shapes. Use your fingers, a brush or a wad of cotton to place dark ink or water-based paint on the paper. Trace the movements of a storm in the still wet, dark color. Let some white paper show through. It will add light to the dark sky. Work quickly and stop just as soon as you get a good effect. You may do several color sketches. Do not overwork a "good thing." Your painting of a stormy sky should be part accident, part planned, and all your own.

ABOUT THE ARTIST

El Greco
(Domenicos
Theotocopoulos)
1548–1614

El Greco is one of the great artists of Spain but he was born on the Greek island of Crete. This explains the name that he is known by, El Greco, which means "The Greek." His art is typical of 16th-century Spain. Not only is it deeply religious, but it is fiercely independent, serious and gay, practical and mysterious.

When El Greco was a young artist he left Greece and went to Italy. This was the time of the Renaissance when Italy was the hub of the art world. El Greco was especially attracted to the works of the Italian artists, Titian and Tintoretto. He remembered the art of his Greek homeland. To this, he added the colors of the Italian painters.

After a few years in Italy, El Greco left for Spain. He settled in Toledo where he spent the rest of his life. There the artist found his true home; his work forever after remained completely Spanish.

ABOUT THE PAINTING

"Rouen Cathedral, West Façade, Sunlight," Monet

1840–1926

This is one of 20 paintings Monet made of the great Gothic Cathedral of Rouen in France. Each of the 20 paintings shows a different time of day, from early morning to sunset. This artist was so anxious to picture Nature that a serious problem for him was noting changes in sunlight during the day and from day to day. Nature would not remain still long enough for him to faithfully capture its effects.

This (like all 20 paintings) shows Monet's love of the effect of light on a surface and his skill in painting pure light. Yet Monet was an artist—not a scientist. He selected subjects that delighted his eye and expressed his ideal of beauty. He created his own images, but did not change reality. Here you can see how he faithfully reproduced Gothic arches, the soaring towers, pointed spires, and the sculptured stone façade that typify the Gothic style of architecture. Still, he transformed the subject by his imagination.

When you look at this painting, can you almost "feel" the stones? Even though the stones seem to be as delicate as lace, do you still get the impression that this is a great and strong building? Why do you think the artist made the small dark figures in the lower left corner of the painting?

Notice how the colors seem to shine and reflect the light. Although most of the colors are pale, Monet used some darker colors to suggest the heavy doorways, towers, and windows. Why do you think he might have done this? To emphasize them? Or to emphasize the large, light-struck areas? Perhaps this is not a painting about a cathedral at all. Do you think that the real subject is light?

Look at El Greco's "View of Toledo" on page 9. Do you see the cathedral in the middle of the painting? How is it different from Monet's cathedral? In which painting do you see stronger contrasts in color? In which one do colors seem to disappear? Which painting reflects a serious and thoughtful mood? a quiet, peaceful mood?

When Monet was young, he began to paint out-of-doors and record his on-the-spot impressions. In time, he met other artists who painted in the same bright, light colors of Nature and who used small strokes of broken color to paint their quick impressions. This style later became known as Impressionism.

Louvre, Paris.

"THE BREAKFAST TABLE"

12

"THE SEINE AT GIVERNEY"

In 1863, Monet and his fellow Impressionists were not allowed to show their work at an official exhibition of art. They held their own exhibition, called the *Salon des Refusés*, which means "Show of the Refused." This brought the work of Monet and his friends to the attention of the whole art world.

"Rouen Cathedral" typified the happy view of life of the Impressionists. Monet also loved the sea and painted cliffs, water, and fishing boats, as well as trees, haystacks, and landscapes. His greatest love was his "water garden," where he created pictures of water lilies and expressed his joy in simply being alive.

"HAYSTACKS IN WINTER"

Just as Monet and his friends had attacked the traditional painters who worked in studios and followed rules, a new generation of French painters attacked the Impressionists. Monet, although still a famous artist, was no longer in the limelight. Today, some 50 years after his death, Monet's work again enjoys the respect and attention of the many people who admire beautiful paintings.

Try This

The Impressionists pictured forms as seen at a quick glance. They did not show exact details. Ideas were often only suggested, and imagination completed the image. As an example, notice how he has painted the small figures in the lower left-hand corner of "Rouen Cathedral." Try drawing a few small figures, merely suggesting the basic form of the head, body and legs.

Now try giving an *impression* of a figure or figures. If the shapes you have created are easy to identify as people, you have succeeded.

Try This

The cathedral that Monet painted is one of the great examples of the Gothic style of architecture. Notice the pointed arch that leads the eye upwards. Sketch several Gothic arches.

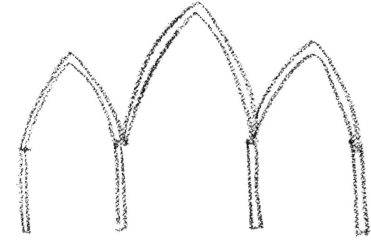

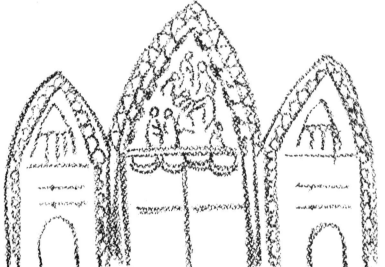

Then add details to suggest carved figures and ornaments. Do not make them carefully detailed. Keep them in the style of the Impressionists.

——— ABOUT THE ARTIST ———

Claude Monet. 1840–1926

When Monet was a child of five, his family moved to Normandy on the coast of France. He hated school, loved the water, and spent most of his time roaming along the beaches. By the time he was 15, he was known for his funny drawings. His work became popular and sold quickly. Monet once said, "Had I gone on like that, I'd be a millionaire today."

As it was, Monet had many problems in his life, including lack of money and a sick wife. One year after his second son was born, Monet's wife died. In time, he married again, and in his later years the artist enjoyed a peaceful family life.

Around 1908, the painter began to grow blind and hardly ever left his garden. But this did not stop him. Monet painted some of his greatest works in his garden among the water lilies. He was commissioned to produce a large series of paintings by the French people, and this led to an important exhibition of his work.

Monet died at Giverny, France, on December 5, 1926, at the age of 86. He is remembered by many as an elderly man painting in the garden that he loved, at peace with himself and the world.

"Girl with a Hoop," Renoir

1844–1919

This wide-eyed girl is typical of the children that the artist Renoir created on canvas. The child is posing for the artist, and she has obviously dressed up for the occasion in a delicate white dress with a beautiful blue sash. This painting permits us to share Renoir's joy in childhood.

Color was Renoir's special delight. The blues, greens, and pale shadows reflect the colors that he used in this period of his career. Note the soft, blurred, almost melting edges of the forms. The garden path is a pale, glowing area that provides a suitable background for the figure. Notice the upper right-hand area of the painting. The freely brushed shrubs, leaves, and flowers suggest the motion of the wind. Renoir suggested depth, or perspective, with a darker colored background.

Do you feel that this is a peaceful scene? that the little girl is happy? If you do, do you know why? Do you think it might be because

of the soft colors, the repeated curves, or the suggestion of rounded forms? Do you think the painting is realistic? Or do you think Renoir has made a picture of an ideal? Some people might find the child too sweet and charming; however, Renoir paints so beautifully that for a brief moment, we are taken in by this image of childhood.

Turn to "Puppet Show" by Paul Klee on page 21 and compare it with "Girl with a Hoop." These two paintings both present views of childhood. How do you think they are alike? How are they different? Which one do you feel is the closest to the truth? Compare the use of colors in these two paintings. Although "Puppet Show" is very dark, does it seem gloomy to you? If not, do you think it might be because the dark background makes the bright colors stand out? Do you prefer the sunny feeling in "Girl with a Hoop," or the brightly striped effect in "Puppet Show"?

Renoir belonged to the Impressionist group of painters. He used light colors, applied in short, broken strokes, and he pictured a world of dancing couples, gay picnics and sun-filled gardens. He preferred painting people to landscapes, and much of his work is filled with solid, frolicking ladies. His work was widely exhibited and collectors became eager to buy it. Renoir was able to earn a comfortable living by painting portraits that pictured charming, joyful, and well-to-do people.

Renoir travelled in Italy, and was influenced there by the work of the Renaissance painter,

Louvre, Paris.

"DANCE AT THE MOULIN DE LA GALETTE"

Painted in about 1885. 49½ × 30⅜ in. (126 × 77 cm.). Oil on Canvas. National Gallery of Art, Washington, D.C. Chester Dale Collection.

"GIRL WITH A HOOP," Pierre Auguste Renoir.

"UMBRELLAS"

National Gallery, London.

Raphael. Renoir's art became more solid, his outlines clearer, and his figures more carefully drawn. Towards the end of his career, another change in his style took place. Renoir expressed his personal view of "the good life" in a more moving or dynamic way. He used darker and more glowing colors, and he got more perspective into his work.

As Renoir grew older, he became paralyzed by rheumatism. However, his work continued to mirror his optimistic view of life. His wife, children, and a servant, Gabrielle, were willing models. Renoir, like his friend Monet, spent his last years in his garden. His paintings celebrated youth and gaiety even when illness made it so painful for him to hold a brush that he had to have it tied to his hand.

Try This

Renoir created an illusion of depth by making distant things smaller and placing them at the top of the painting. Notice that the tree trunk in "Girl with a Hoop" is smaller than the stick the girl is holding. The tree is also placed at the top of the picture. This is how the artist created a feeling of distance. Experiment with this effect in your own paintings.

ABOUT THE ARTIST

Pierre Auguste Renoir 1841–1919

Renoir was the son of a French tailor who had a large family to support. At the age of 13, young Renoir left school and was apprenticed to a porcelain painter. The boy was taught to paint bouquets of flowers and small figures on china dishes. Renoir learned quickly, but he was not happy with this routine work. He often visited the Louvre Museum in Paris and copied the work of the early Greek and Roman

sculptors. In time, Renoir saved enough money to enroll in an art class.

The story of Renoir's life follows a traditional pattern. A poor boy works hard and saves his money to attend school where he finds his true vocation. He makes his fortune, marries, and lives happily ever after.

Renoir was neither an experimenter nor a rebel in the field of painting. Yet the appeal that attracted collectors in Renoir's day continues to attract the public to his paintings today. They are often the focus of popular attention in the museums where they are shown. People still enjoy seeing bright colors and happy people.

From "Make Your Own Greeting Cards," by Chester J. Alkema, Sterling Publishing Co. Inc.

Try This

Renoir's art celebrates the joy of life. Try to express your ideas about the happy things in life in a collage. Collect photographs, magazine and newspaper clippings, advertisements, and so on, that illustrate happy times. Arrange your images on a background paper. Try overlapping some shapes and varying the sizes and shapes to create a feeling of depth. Try several arrangements before pasting the parts in place. The completed collage should reflect your personal idea of "the good life."

Try This

Renoir and the other Impressionists used small daubs of color to make their impressions clear. They placed color next to color in very small areas. For example, examine the leaves in the background of "Girl with a Hoop."

Use crayons to experiment with the methods of the Impressionists. Create flowers and shrubs with short strokes of light and dark colors. Do not picture the exact form of leaves and flowers. Merely suggest the forms with a stroke of color.

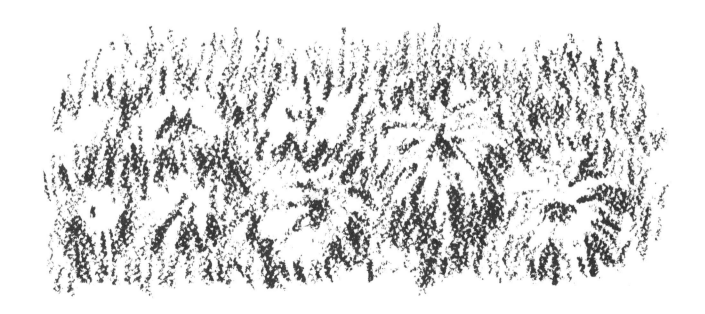

"Puppet Show," Klee

1879–1940

In this painting, the artist Klee (pronounced like *clay*) surprises us with the childlike simplicity of the disconnected images he has included. Notice the child puppeteer. The sun is in her eyes, there is a curl to her lip, and her heart is in the right place. Against the dark background of the puppet stage, we see the sun that shines in many pictures made by children. We also see a window, a door, a striped puppet, a disjointed horned beast, and flowers. When the puzzle is put together, we have all we need for a puppet performance.

Klee's intention was to approach art with childlike simplicity. He allowed his imagination to work freely and did not plan his composition or review the ideas that came to him. Klee explained that he allowed ideas to grow in the same way that Nature allows a creature of the deep sea to grow and change its appearance. He searched for a beautiful design. Notice the perfectly balanced composition, the attractive combination of colors, the dark and light areas, and the clear and simple shapes.

Collection of Mrs. Gertrude Lenart, New York.

"CLOWN"

As a child, the artist often made puppets and staged informal puppet shows. This painting recalls these experiences of his childhood. However, this does not mean that it is *childish*. Klee presents the experiences and ideas as an adult does, but in a style that is characteristic of the drawings of young children.

Do you think that Klee felt sad when he painted the "Puppet Show"? Do you think that the puppeteer is crying? Why do you think that the puppet is lying on its side? Do you think it is because Klee was trying to suggest a lost childhood? Perhaps you think that this is a happy painting. If you do, why?

Compare "Puppet Show" with Goya's "Portrait of Don Manuel" on page 29. The little boy is also surrounded by the treasures of his childhood—his pets. Do you think that these two paintings are similar in other ways? Which painting most closely relates to your childhood? Which style would you choose if

Collection of Felix Klee, Berne.

"STILL LIFE"

Painted in 1923. 20½ × 14 in. (52 × 36 cm.). Gouache. The Klee Foundation, Bern, Switzerland. Permission COSMOPRESS and SPADEM 1973 by French Reproduction Rights, Inc.

"PUPPET SHOW," Paul Klee.

Doetsch-Benziger Collection, Basle.

"LANDSCAPE WITH YELLOW BIRDS"

ready to accept a view of Klee's inner world. The meanings within his work are sometimes difficult to discover. His simple drawings are a disguise for ideas that are often difficult to understand. Remember as you study "Puppet Show" that Paul Klee was a trained artist who *chose* to paint this way.

you wanted to show how you felt about things when you were very young? Can you tell why?

Klee's work has often been compared to doodles completed in the offhand way that you might doodle along the margins of a notebook. The difference between Klee and the everyday doodler lies in the fact that while the doodler is playing, Klee is busy with serious business.

Klee associated with the famous artists of the early 1900's. He was friendly with Marc, Kandinsky, Picasso, and Braque, painters you will meet in other books in this series. He developed a sensitive and playful use of line that made a special appeal to people who were

Uhlmann Collection, Berlin.

"MASK"

ABOUT THE ARTIST
Paul Klee. 1879–1940

Klee was born in Switzerland, the son of a German music teacher and a Swiss mother. He grew up in Berne, but studied art at the Academy in Munich, Germany. While in his early 20's, he travelled to Italy and France, came back, married, and finally settled in Munich, determined to develop an art style of his own. Although he had a firm foundation in drawing and perspective, his work never showed this traditional background.

In 1926, Klee became a professor at the Bauhaus. This was a famous German school that tried to bring together architecture, industrial arts, and the fine arts. He continued to teach and to exhibit his work until 1933 when his work was attacked by Hitler's Nazi government. Klee was forced to leave Germany and returned to Berne, where he continued to work until his death.

Try This

For a moment, try to forget your age. Be a very young child and look at things the way you think the child would. Then draw or paint a picture in a childlike way. It is not easy to forget the things you have learned, so it might help to think of the images that appear in the art of small children. A house, a tree, a flower, boys, girls, and the sun are pictured by children all over the world.

When Paul Klee created the images of childhood, he would usually begin his work with no exact idea in mind. He let the feelings and ideas of childhood take over. You might try to work in the same way.

Try This

Create a "puppet in the news." Cut out the face of a well known person from a newspaper or magazine. Paste the cutout on cardboard or other heavy paper. Do a whole figure or just a head. You might add details of clothing, symbols, and so on. Cut out the figure you have made. On the other side of the figure, add details of clothing, hair, and such, so that the puppet is interesting from both front and back. Attach the figure to a stick. Work the stick to animate the puppet. Now you are ready to present your puppet with a speaking part that goes with the character.

23

"Café Terrace at Night," Van Gogh

1853–1890

This painting was done in Arles in the south of France. Van Gogh set up his easel in the cobblestoned street not far from the café, and enjoyed the bright and busy night scene while he painted. The lights from the café and the shop windows brighten the darkness. The lines of the café terrace, the street, and the rooftops create a feeling of space and carry your eye along, past the café, and on into the distance.

Can you see how the artist's brush moved in the branches of the tree? in the sky? in the texture of the café wall? These broken strokes of color make the surface of the painting seem to vibrate. Notice how the dark blue areas bring out the strong yellow light. Color gives a dramatic feeling to this place. Do you think an artist's view often is more beautiful than the real view?

This painting was done towards the end of the artist's life, at a time when his personal feelings were often angry and unhappy. However, the painting does not show the torture of

Van Gogh's violent and stormy moods. His strong colors and brushwork made him an influence in the painting of today. The feelings he was able to express and the bright colors he used continue to inspire modern artists.

Compare "Café Terrace at Night" with Boccioni's "Forces of a Street" on page 37. Both show busy street scenes, but the artists chose very different ways to express their impressions. Which street would you prefer to visit? Which one do you find most exciting? Do you know why? What do you think the artist Boccioni was trying to show about a street? What do you think Van Gogh was saying about the street he painted? Do you feel that both paintings are happy scenes? If so, why?

Van Gogh's only success was in his painting. His first work, painted in Holland, showed the darkness and sadness of his life and those about him. He painted farmers, weavers, miners, and other people involved in heavy work. Yet, in these somewhat clumsy drawings and paintings, the artist was, for the first time in his life, able to express his feelings.

In 1886, Vincent went to Paris from Holland to visit his brother Theo. While there, he saw the sun-filled paintings of the Impressionists. His imagination was captured by the brightness and joy expressed in these paintings. Also, the city impressed him by its people, activity, and color. Van Gogh's way of painting changed from a dark, gloomy view of the world to a view filled with light.

Two years later, in 1888, Van Gogh went to the south of France and painted out-of-doors

Kröller-Müller Museum, Otterlo.

"THE LOOM"

Painted in 1888. 32¼ × 26 in. (82 × 66 cm.). Oil. Statemuseum Kröller-Müller. Otterlo.

Stedelijk Museum, Amsterdam.
"AT THE CAFÉ TAMBOURIN"

and people. It was at this time that he painted "Café Terrace at Night." His paintings expressed a love of Nature and a joy in life that Van Gogh found only through his art. The unhappiness and loneliness in his life could not be seen in his later work.

Then Van Gogh became seriously ill and entered a hospital where he lived for a year and continued to paint. But he was not mentally strong enough to fight the painful images in his mind and he killed himself.

Kröller-Müller Museum, Otterlo.
"STREET WITH CYPRESSES"

in the bright sunlight. There he captured the vivid yellows and greens of the countryside. The sun itself seemed to blaze in his work. He pictured swirling heavens, sunny streets, starry skies, lively sunflowers, simple indoor scenes,

ABOUT THE ARTIST

Vincent van Gogh
1853–1890

The artist was born in The Netherlands, the son of a minister, and one of six children. Vincent was always different from the others— a shy, unhappy boy who spent most of his time alone. His only real friend was his youngest brother, Theo.

At the age of 16, Vincent went to work as a salesman in an art gallery. He stayed at the job for several years, but in time lost interest in his work. Some time later, he tried to become a minister, but he could not complete the difficult studies for the ministry. He offered to work for his church and was sent to aid the miners of the Borinage, a poor mining section in Belgium.

Filled with good intentions, but poorly equipped to help others, Van Gogh gave until he had nothing left. He became ill, but remained

until the church authorities sent him home. Now 27 years old, Vincent van Gogh was still a failure. Then he began to draw. For the next 10 years, until his death, art was his only interest.

Van Gogh's ability was not recognized until after his death. During his lifetime, his great need to create art was encouraged only by the love and financial support provided by his brother Theo, who became an art dealer. Even though Van Gogh was unable to sell his works during the 10 years that he spent as a painter, Theo's faith in his ability never changed.

Try This

You have observed the artist's brush strokes in "Café Terrace at Night." Now create a row of evergreen trees. Let the direction of each line you make follow the direction suggested by the branches of the tree. It might help you to think of these trees as triangles.

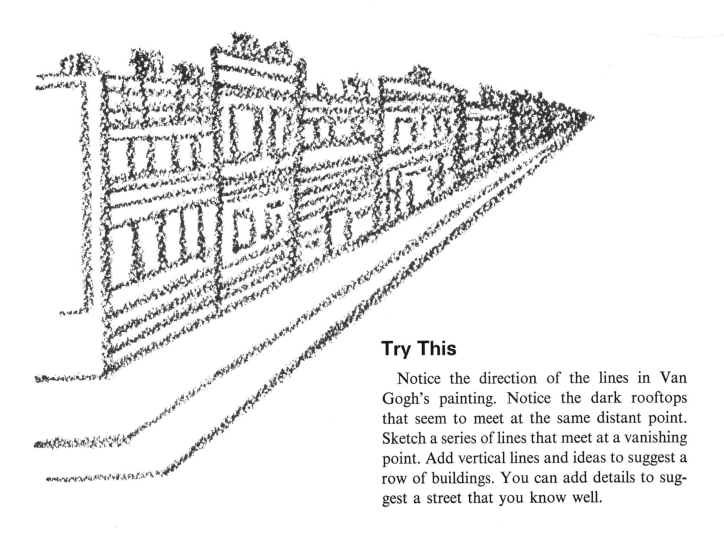

Try This

Notice the direction of the lines in Van Gogh's painting. Notice the dark rooftops that seem to meet at the same distant point. Sketch a series of lines that meet at a vanishing point. Add vertical lines and ideas to suggest a row of buildings. You can add details to suggest a street that you know well.

"Portrait of Don Manuel," Goya

1746–1826

Don Manuel, the son of a Spanish nobleman, is dressed in the elegant style of his day as he poses for the artist. The little boy is surrounded by his pets. The magpie which he is holding by a string can do simple tricks, such as picking up the letter. A cage of small birds and three cats complete the picture. (You might miss the third cat unless you look carefully!)

Notice how the artist draws our attention immediately to the child's pale face. His dark hair stands out against the brightly lit background. Then we move on to the beautiful red suit with the satin sash and delicate lace bow. Does the painting seem to glow to you? Do you think it might be because of the strong contrasts of light and dark colors? Notice how the shadows and large areas are barely suggested, while the artist took great pains to show details such as the lace and the bird-cage.

Does this seem like a peaceful scene to you? Does the boy look happy? Notice the way the large black-and-white cat is staring at the magpie. Some people believe that Goya painted the cat's evil expression as a way of speaking out about the evils of his day.

Compare this painting of a child with Renoir's "Girl with a Hoop" on page 17. Do you think that both artists showed their love for children in these paintings? If you do, can you explain why? Why do you think that both artists placed their child model in the very middle of the painting? Even though these children are dressed in the styles of two different centuries, can you find similarities in parts of their clothing?

This portrait of Don Manuel was made at the start of Goya's career when he was a painter in the King's Court. He began in the tradition of storytelling and, like other artists of his time, his paintings, such as "The Pottery Seller," were made for tapestries. For this reason, much of his early art is lacking in detail, since it was to be adapted into a tapestry.

Prado, Madrid.

"THE POTTERY SELLER"

"PORTRAIT OF DON MANUEL OSORIO DE ZUNIGA," Francisco Goya.

Prado, Madrid.

"CHARLES IV AND HIS FAMILY"
(Detail)

Engraving from the Caprichos.

"WHY ARE THEY HIDING ?"

At the height of his career, Goya used very warm and unusual color combinations. In time, along with his own decline in health and the political situation in Spain, Goya's art changed. He used less and less color and more black, white, and brown, and his paintings showed the horrors of war. He no longer painted the elegant and noble society of the Court. Dreamlike images and nightmarish figures appeared in his work.

These paintings were symbolic of Goya's critical feelings about what was going on round him. When civil war raged in Madrid, the artist no longer felt safe at home. He fled to France, and died in exile, a lonely, old man.

"THE GIANT"

"THE THIRD OF MAY"

Prado, Madrid.

Try This

Create a self-portrait. Goya expressed the personality as well as the outward appearance of little Don Manuel. You, too, can express a personality in a portrait. Think about yourself—your hobbies, activities, and ideals.

Collect cutouts that suggest "you," and make a collage. Also use fabrics, yarn, and other bits and pieces. Arrange your collection to suggest a face, a figure or a design that in some way expresses *you*. Glue the parts to a background paper, and add lines if you want to make your idea clearer.

ABOUT THE ARTIST

Francisco
Goya
1746–1828

"SELF
PORTRAIT"

Francisco Goya's full name was Francisco José de Goya y Lucientes. He was born in the small village of Fuendetodos in the Aragon area of Spain. In 1760, the family moved to Zaragoza, and Francisco attended a convent school. He took drawing lessons at this time.

When he was 17, Goya was sent to Madrid and apprenticed to Francisco Bayeu, a painter in the Court of the King. Soon after, he travelled to Italy for further studies. He returned to Madrid, married Bayeu's sister, and was soon commissioned by the Court to paint scenes for tapestries.

Success and wealth came rapidly, and he became very popular as a portrait painter. Then, in 1792, Goya became very ill and lost his hearing. From that time on, his painting changed and reflected the unhappiness in his own life and life round him. He lived outside Madrid in a house known as *La Quinta del Sordo* (The House of the Deaf). His mental health failed, and the artist who began his career painting lovely courtly portraits such as that of little Don Manuel, ended his career painting horrible creatures of his imagination.

ABOUT THE PAINTING

"Woman with Mango," Gauguin

1848–1903

This painting was made on the little tropical island of Tahiti in the South Pacific where the French artist Gauguin searched for a simple life and tried to forget "all the evils of the past." Gauguin tried to leave civilization behind and think simply. "You do not need to seek poetry there. It is there for all to see." The poetry that Gauguin saw in Tahiti is expressed in this painting about a beautiful young woman.

Notice the soft curves of the woman's dress, her long hair adorned with flowers, her graceful pose, and calm glance. Do you like the feeling that you get from this painting? Do the colors that the artist used suggest a warm, tropical place to you? Does this painting show a closeness of the woman with Nature? How?

"Woman with Mango" represents Gauguin's

Municipal Museum, Amsterdam.

"VAN GOGH PAINTING SUNFLOWERS"

ideal of human love and rejection of the greed and hatred that exist in the world. Gauguin hated the ambitions of men. He said, "A terrible ordeal is in store in Europe for the coming generation: the Kingdom of Gold." Before he went to Tahiti, Gauguin's paintings echoed those of the Impressionists. Then he began to move from place to place in search of new ways to express his ideas. He was one of a group of artists who called themselves Symbolists. They painted images from imagination and showed feelings such as love, despair, devotion, and faith.

Gauguin began to use color with no likeness to Nature. Trees might be painted red, hills yellow. Color was decided by his personal feelings as an artist. The shapes of Nature and people were changed in the same way. Notice the simply painted shapes in the woman's face. Head, shoulders, and arms are turned to

"STILL LIFE WITH APPLES"

ABOUT THE ARTIST

Paul Gauguin
1848–1903

Gauguin was born in Paris. He spent several years in Peru as a young man, then returned to France and joined the Merchant Navy. When he returned to civilian life, he worked in the office of a stockbroker in Paris. When 25 years old, he married a wealthy Danish girl and, in time, he became successful in business and the father of a large family.

During these years, Gauguin started to paint as a hobby. He followed the ideas of the Impressionists and by the time he was 32, he began exhibiting his paintings with them. Soon he decided to devote all of his time to painting. In a short time, his fortune went downhill. His earnings in business gone, he took up work as a billposter during a cold winter and from then on began a new life as a wanderer.

Gauguin had an odd personality. He could not get along with his fellow artists and friends. He had a violent fight with his friend Vincent van Gogh, which resulted in Van Gogh's cutting off his own ear. Ill health, poverty, and a dislike for society led Gauguin to seek refuge in a faraway place. In 1891, when he was 43, he went to Tahiti. There, in spite of great poverty, dreadful illness, and a constant fight with the authorities, Gauguin found the ideas for his great works. Among the people of Tahiti, Gauguin was able to find the friendship and the unselfish love that he needed.

The artist returned to France for a short time, but he was unhappy and unable to adjust to the needs of European civilization. After becoming ill once again, he returned to the South Pacific in a last effort to find peace, and died soon after.

repeat graceful curves. The mass of her figure is only suggested. The artist does not need to show exactly how things appear; yet, "Woman with Mango" is a clear, easily understood painting.

Notice the contrasting colors—blue and orange-yellow, the pattern of dark and light, the large areas of flat color. Large flower shapes are repeated in the background and add interest to the composition. Gauguin once

Albright Gallery, Buffalo.

"YELLOW CHRIST"

Öffentliche Kunstsammlung, Basle.

"TA MATETE"

said, "Let everything about you breathe the calm and peace of the soul." Do you think that this painting expresses this ideal?

Both Gauguin and Paul Klee sought to approach painting in the most simple, almost childlike, way as possible. Compare "Woman with Mango" with Klee's "Puppet Show" on page 21. Which artist do you think has been most successful in his aim? Even though Klee painted in what seems to be the style of a child, do you find his painting more difficult to understand? Or do the large flat shapes and unusual colors of the Gauguin painting seem strange and unreal to you? Do you know which painting appeals to you the most and why? If you do not like either painting, can you explain your reasons?

Try This

Gauguin used large areas of color for his shapes. Draw a figure using the flat, simple shapes suggested by the Gauguin painting, but make sure your figure is an "original." Then, select color pages from a magazine, and cut and paste shapes on your drawing to complete the figure.

Try This

Sketch two curved lines to suggest a bowl. Then fill the bowl with fruit and add shading to highlight the forms. Do this by laying on

several pencil lines where you want shadows. Let the lines follow the form of the object. Then use your finger to rub the pencil lines into a soft shadow. Have the movement of your finger follow the form of the object you draw. As you "feel" your way round the sketched form, you will create a feeling of weight or mass.

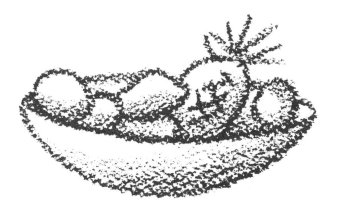

"Forces of a Street," Boccioni

1882–1916

This painting is about the lights, movement, color, and excitement of a city street. The artist did not show the actual appearance of the buildings, street and people; instead, he pictured his idea of the forces that filled the air and surrounded the people and objects. In "Forces of a Street," the artist expresses through art a personal feeling that he could not share through words.

Your eye is led into space by lines that seem to go back to a vanishing point near the top of the painting. Broken lines, triangles, and other straight-edged shapes break up the push into space suggested by the crossing lines. Rays of bright light form arches that cover the city street. The downward push of

"THE STREET PAVERS"

the lights goes into the space between the tall buildings.

Have you ever felt the excitement in a busy city street at night without knowing exactly what force it is that causes the excitement? Does this painting express your feelings about it? What things do you recognize in this abstract, or unrealistic, painting? Can you find figures of people? Cars? Buildings? Streetlights?

Turn to El Greco's "View of Toledo" on page 9 and compare his ideas and feelings about a city with Boccioni's. Do you think that El Greco painted his city exactly as he saw it? Or do you think he too changed the scene according to his own ideas and imagination? Do you think that both paintings show the artists' feelings towards cities? Why do you think that El Greco used curved and flowing lines and Boccioni used straight lines and angles? Does the El Greco suggest movement? Which painting seems happy to you? Which one seems gloomy? Compare the colors in both paintings. Are they similar? How did El Greco show people in comparison with the way in which Boccioni painted them? Small? Important? Unimportant?

The artist Boccioni felt the changes brought about by the Machine Age. He observed the ways in which machines were changing the world and he felt that one day machines would rule the lives of men. Boccioni expressed power and energy in his art, but they were man-made. El Greco also was showing power and energy, but they were the forces of

"FORCES OF A STREET," Umberto Boccioni.

Painted in 1911. 39¾ × 31½ in. (100 × 80 cm.). Oil on Canvas. Collection, Dr. Paul Hanggi, Basle.

37

"SELF PORTRAIT"

Nature. His painting of the city of Toledo expressed his feeling of the overpowering forces of Nature, not machines. He could not have then dreamed of the mechanized age in which we live today.

Boccioni tried to show force by experimenting with repeated lines and overlapping shapes. He also invented streamlined forms in sculpture of the human figure, and even suggested using glass and plastic for sculpture. Boccioni was ahead of today's sculptors when he suggested using "a little motor" to create movement in a work of art.

ABOUT THE ARTIST

Umberto Boccioni
1882–1916

Boccioni is a 20th-century Italian artist. As a young man, he painted pictures that were realistic. Later, he became the leader of a group of artists who believed that Italian art had imitated the old masters for too long. They called themselves "Futurists" to explain their break with the past and their interest in the future. Their idea was to express the movement, forces, and high speeds that surround modern man. Boccioni and his friends publicized their ideas with demonstrations, meetings, publications, and exhibitions.

Boccioni and the other Futurists, unlike most men of art, praised violence and war. However, all of the members of the Futurist group did not continue with these ideas after World War I. Those men who survived the war went in various other artistic directions. Boccioni was killed in a fall from a horse at the age of 34. Although he lived before man sent a rocket to the moon, Boccioni was propelled into space by his imagination.

Try This

Repeated lines suggest motion in a certain direction. Repeat lines that can be straight, slanted, angular, or curved. Notice the push of the movement suggested by your pattern of lines. Use the most successful experiment to create a design.

Try This

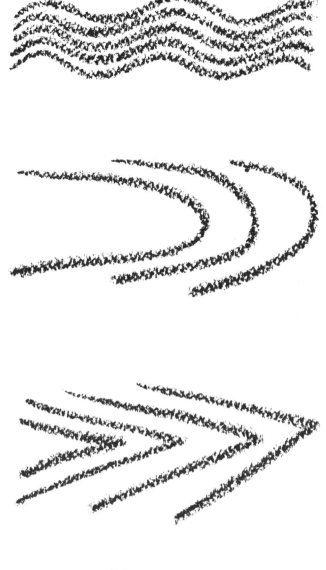

Boccioni found beauty in city lights, cars, and tall buildings just as others might find beauty in hills, trees, and sky. Some people find beauty in the lines and shapes of a machine, such as the young artist who made the drawing of the motorcycle shown here. He obviously prefers machines to landscapes, but this love for a machine is not always connected to the work a machine can do. It is often connected to the appearance of the machine.

Explore the design of a machine by sketching a car or bicycle. Illustrate a regular model or create a fantastic "Futuristic" machine. You might also use an advertisement for a car as an inspiration for invention. Paste the cutout ad on a background paper. Use a soft-tipped ink marker to add imaginative details to the original model.

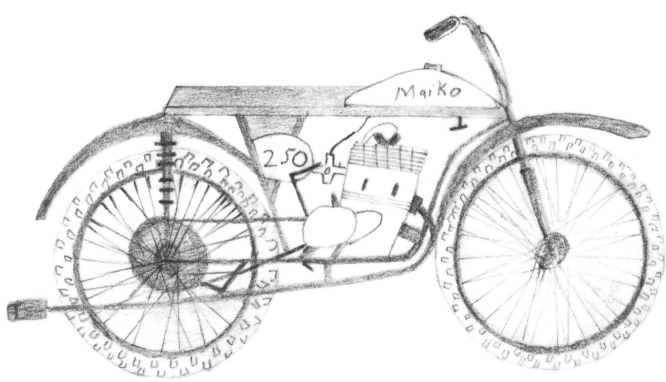

Index